The Official Fanbook

John Mosby

BOXTREE

Acknowledgements

I would like to thank everyone connected with *Barb Wire* who gave their time in interviews for this book and also: Rich Young at Dark Horse Comics, Stacy Bell at PolyGram, Rosanna Norton for permission to reprint her designs, Davod & Co. at Odyssey (Leeds), Tony Earnshaw at the *Yorkshire Post*, Mike Hadley (at The Mirtle), Jon Courtenay Grimwood, Steve Holland and, of course, all at Boxtree. Many thanks also to Paul H.Birch, David Richardson, all at *Sci-fi Universe* for their respective 'breaks'.

For Peter, Angela, Steven and Roy who will be pleased, and David Shearing, who would have been.

First published in 1996 by Boxtree Ltd, Broadwall House, 21 Broadwall, London SE1 9PL

Barb Wire movie script by Chuck Pfarrer and Adam Rifkin

10 9 8 7 6 5 4 3 2 1

Studio photography by Steve Wayda
On-set production photography Wren Maloney

Designed by Dan Newman

Reproduction by Jade Reprographics Ltd, Essex.

Printed and bound in Great Britain by Cambus Litho Ltd, East Kilbride.

ISBN: 0 7522 0194 8
A CIP catalogue entry for this book is available from the British Library

CONTENTS

INTRODUCTION

Barb Wire. Call her when you need help, call her when you need fire-power, just don't call her 'Babe'!

If there's one person you don't want tracking you down, it's Steel Harbor's favourite bounty-hunter. But just who is Barb Wire?

Barbara 'Barb' Kopetski is a lady with a shady past and an equally shadowy present. As well as being a part-time bounty-hunter she is also the proprietress of the famous (or perhaps infamous) Hammerhead Bar and Grille, Steel Harbor's most 'happening' night-spot. In a run-down, crime-ridden place like Steel Harbor that may not mean too much. Between running the bar, capturing escaped felons and avoiding the violent brawls which break out all too often...Barb Wire often has her hands full.

Now, they're about to get fuller.

Barb Wire, previously one of Dark Horse Comics' successful stable of comic-book characters, is now transferring to the silver screen in a big-budget action movie. Taking the role of the heroine is none other than *Baywatch* star Pamela Anderson in her first big-budget movie. Along for the ride is rising star, New Zealander, Temeura Morrison (as the mysterious Axel Hood), who is best known for his role in *Once Were Warriors*, and a host of other characters guaranteed to provide a strong assortment of allies and villains. But in a place like Steel Harbor your friends and enemies may just be the people you haven't killed yet!

In the following pages we'll be taking a look at the movie, the characters, the stars, the original comic. We'll be talking exclusively with Chris Warner, the man who first created Barb Wire. Find out what the actors behind the big screen characters have to say about the movie. Hear about the problems that the film-makers had, and the solutions they came up

with. And see how everything finally came together for *Barb Wire: The Movie.*

So sit down, buckle up and beware of low-flying objects. Please deposit your fire-arms at the door and have your identification ready. You're about to enter Steel Harbor's foremost drinking establishment and meet its array of colourful characters. Don't cause any trouble or you'll have the owner to answer to.

You're in for the ride of your life with a lady called Barb Wire. It's an experience you'll never forget. Just remember, whatever you do....

don't call her 'Babe'!

Chapter 1

BARB WIRE: THE MOVIE

The story in words and pictures!

Imagine a world only a few years away. Sometime in the near future...a dark future where you can't trust anyone but yourself – and that's just on a good day! Welcome to Steel Harbor, in what's left of the old USA. Welcome to the world of Barb Wire...

FADE IN: *Montage of images. Wheat blowing in the wind, picturesque tower blocks against a blue sky. The Statue of Liberty...explodes.*

Drum roll...the first strains of the American National Anthem...

"In 1858 Abraham Lincoln said 'A house divided against itself cannot stand.' One hundred and fifty years later the house fell...

"It was impossible to conceive. The tragedy, the horror of a second American civil war. The United States government was overthrown from within. The reins of power were seized by a group calling itself the Congressional Directorate. They suspended the Constitution in the name of new justice and a mighty war began.

"The conquerors were swift. Anarchy reigned. America had become a third world. The hope of a better tomorrow seemed impossible for the home of the brave. The war raged from sea to sea, every city under siege except for one. Mandated by the United Nations as a demilitarised, cease-fire zone, this city stood alone...neutral turf. They call it Steel Harbor!"

So begins the big screen version of *Barb Wire*, the image of the American Star-Spangled Banner burning in the wind fading to the image of a lone biker roaring down the litter-strewn, vandalised streets. This is the world of Barb Wire, and unlike the woman on the motorcycle, it's not a pretty sight.

Meanwhile, in a dark and even more threatening place, Colonel Victor Pryzer of the Congressional Directorate is enjoying his favourite hobby. Torture. His sinister equipment is capable of reading the images in people's brains. His prisoner is trying to resist, but to no avail. "Don't think of an elephant," Pryzer tells her. An elephant appears on the viewscreen. Ah, manipulating the mind is such a wonderful pastime for the Colonel! Finally his captive breaks down and gives Pryzer the information he wants. A pair of retinal contact lenses are en route to Steel Harbor, to be picked up by the one of the resistance's most enigmatic leaders, Dr Corrina Devonshire, otherwise known as the inspirational

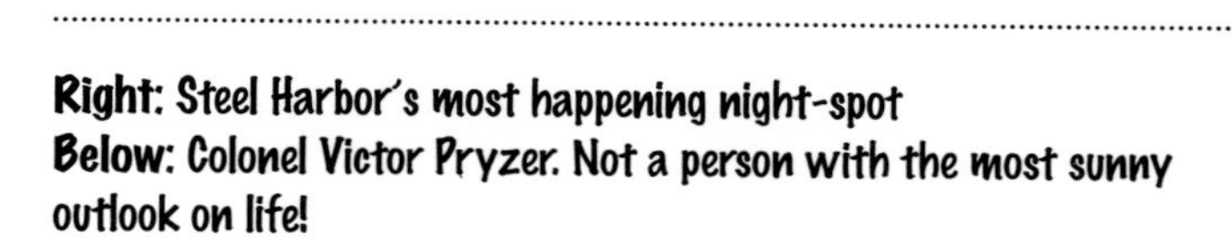
Right: Steel Harbor's most happening night-spot
Below: Colonel Victor Pryzer. Not a person with the most sunny outlook on life!

Cora D. The fugitive knows too many of the Directorate's secrets. One secret in particular could be the deciding factor in who wins the war, and now the doctor is on the run, carrying with her the information that Pryzer and the Directorate would kill to recover. The lenses are to be picked up from a low-life named William Krebs. Pryzer decides to alert the relevant local authority. He cannot afford to let Cora D escape...or live.

Steel Harbor's favourite Bar and Grille (and most likely the only one left standing given the surroundings) is the Hammerhead bar, owned by the unforgettable Barb Wire. The bar and the woman are something of legend. There are rumours and quiet, hesitant talk in the shadows that there is a lot more to Barb than meets the eye. And that's saying something. One of the more credible rumours is that she was once a freedom fighter. But no-one can prove anything and Barb is not a person likely to volunteer the information.

Nowadays Barb spends her time running the bar with her blind younger brother, Charlie (whose talent for engineering and tinkering allows Barb to have some of the most creative and destructive weapons around). What does a bar-owner need with the latest technology? Well, Barb also has a nice side-line as a bounty hunter. She has declared herself as neutral as the city in which she makes her home. However, if you're a customer who won't pay up, or a bail-jumper on the run, don't expect any soft treatment. It's a tough city in tough times and Barb is more than willing to break a few heads if it's necessary. But tonight she can be found, if she wants to be found, in the office above the club.

Meanwhile, down on the sea-front, two mysterious figures are arriving in Steel Harbor. One is a brooding, heavily-built figure. The other is an elegant young black woman. They are met by the resistance who promise to take them to Krebs. Everything goes haywire when Customs stops the car. A shoot-out ensues and the fugitives are forced to abandon the car. Guns blazing behind them, the couple disappear into the night.

One of the figures is a surgically altered Cora D, unrecognisable to those who knew her before. The only way to positively identify her would be to scan the unique retinal pattern of her eyes. That little loop-hole is why she's here in Steel Harbor. The other figure is a man named Axel Hood, a man who has more than a few past connections to a woman named Barb Wire. That big loop-hole is why he's here!

Axel Hood and Cora D, wanted dead or alive...preferably dead

With a little help from her friends, Curly (above) and her blind brother Charlie (right)

Back at the Hammerhead, it's a typically busy night. Customers are lining up to get in, some are even trying to bribe their way in...unsuccessfully. Inside, Curly, the Hammerhead's frenetic head waiter, is trying to keep things running smoothly – no mean achievement given the usual conditions. When Barb is 'indisposed', Curly usually takes the messages and most of the flak. Tonight an elderly senator is requesting Barb to join him and his four female companions for a drink. In another corner a shady deal is going down, a suitcase is quickly closed and a contract is agreed. Curly continues his rounds and comes across a man getting a tattoo of Barb on his chest. If the man can't have her in the flesh, he'll at least have her *on* the flesh. A few minutes later, a visiting sheik repeats his offer to pay Barb a considerable sum for removing the legs of his ex-partner. Barb has already declined the invitation but the sheik won't take no for an answer. Until, that is, he meets Camille. Camille is a Rottweiler with as much attitude as her owner. A quick growl and the Sheik is convinced to let the matter drop.

Hood has come to Steel Harbor because he is desperate. He'd have to be: he knows all too well that Barb probably won't be overjoyed to see him again. In fact, she'll probably be tempted to shoot him on the spot – and that's just if she's in a good mood! But he needs urgent help and he knows that the one person who can provide that help is Barb. Axel is helping Cora D get to Canada where she must warn the Truce Commission that the Congressional forces are about to release a deadly new biological weapon which will make the atrocities committed so far seem like bruises and scrapes. Thousands will die if Cora D and Hood fail. Axel knows that Barb has contacts in the darker, dirtier parts of Steel Harbor, but also has a good rapport with both the resistance and Congressional leaders. Most importantly Barb may be able to obtain the retinal contact lenses that will complete Cora's disguise and help her make it across the border.

Charlie Kopetski, as usual, is downing enough alcohol to float the average tanker. He's currently working on 'two tall ones'. One's a double bourbon,

the other is an attractive redhead. Being blind – as well as blind drunk – he fails to notice that the redhead is tired of the chat-up lines and heads back to the action further in the club. He continues with his one-sided conversation. Curly arrives and notes the ridiculous situation. Charlie asks the barkeep for another drink, but Curly signals that Barb's younger brother has already had enough. Charlie smiles. He doesn't need to see Curly to know the routine.

Curly goes up to Barb's office to see if the week's paychecks are going to be late...again.

CURLY: *Boss, is this a good time to talk about the payroll?*

BARB: *No...What's tonight's traffic like?*

CURLY: *Normal Thursday. The usual. The lowest of the bottomfeeders, the highest of the elite and every shade of gray in between, plus some U.N. troopers blowing off a little steam.*

BARB: *Tell them no grenades this time!*

Yep, the business is not cheap to run. What with breakages and bribes to officials such as Alexander Willis (the totally corrupt Chief of Police) costs can run high, even before she can pay Curly. On nights like this Barb is prone to take on the tracking down of bail-jumpers. After all, sleazy characters like bail-bondsman Thomas Schmitz are willing to pay good money for their recapture. Tonight, Barb is hired to bring in another scum-bag. His name: William Krebs.

In her own sweet way, which – in this case – means her masquerading as a street-walker, Barb tricks her way into the apartment next door to Krebs's room, an excellent location to spring her trap. It's all very easy. Maybe a little too easy: you just knew there had to be a catch...

Unfortunately no-one told Barb that the guy was being watched and protected. Two unofficial police 'bodyguards' make her job a little more difficult than usual. They are well-trained and all too eager to take her on. To their credit they try hard, but the end was never really in doubt. Barb Wire almost has to break a sweat – and wouldn't you just know it, she broke

her nail. One of the guards finds himself launched through the window, with no parachute to slow his descent to the pavement far below. But, hey, it was really his own fault: he called her 'Babe'. No-one, but *no-one* calls Barb 'Babe'. At least not if they want to live!

Barb delivers Krebs to Schmitz's office and negotiates (what she considers) a good deal for her night's work. Little does she know that Schmitz has information that makes Krebs extremely valuable. If Barb had any idea of Krebs's real value to Schmitz, she'd have multiplied her fee by a thousand. It would still have been worthwhile to Schmitz. But Barb, as yet, has no idea of the cycle of events that are already underway and the events that she herself has set in motion. But she will soon...

SCHMITZ: *It's been a pleasure doing business...*
BARB: *If it were a pleasure, Schmitz, I'd charge more!*

Barb heads back to the Hammerhead to entertain the clubbers. However, it's not long before some party-poopers arrive. Willis, Steel Harbor's 'relevant authority', decides that he'll give the Hammerhead a routine inspection. He's also a little miffed. Someone, it seems, has sprung one of his contacts from protective custody and killed two of the men guarding him. The contact's name was Krebs and now Willis is

Above: Special Delivery for Mr Schmitz – cash up front
Below: Willis provides 'protection'

none too pleased at the idea of Colonel Pryzer coming to Steel Harbor to take matters into his own hands. It's been a bad day all round and Willis is determined that something is going to go his way.

Willis has come looking for answers, hoping that Barb (or one of her customers) can shed light on the abduction. Little does he realise how close the culprit actually is. He begins to check the retinal scans of some of Barb's clientele. Naturally, most of the patrons have warrants outstanding and criminal records longer than their right arm. If things progressed this way the Hammerhead audience could quickly be reduced to single figures. Barb intervenes. As usual, Willis will settle for a bribe from Barb to leave the customers alone. Willis isn't bad, he's just greedy, and nights like this have become a regular occurrence. It's simply considered 'good business' for both Willis and Barb's sake. It stops the atmosphere getting too heavy.

Willis leaves without the information he was looking for, but several credits richer.

The atmosphere is about to get distinctly heavier. After Willis and his troops have finished their 'inspection', Axel and Cora D arrive at the club. Across the smoke and neon lights, Barb catches sight of Axel. Memories come flooding back, but Barb has no time for memories. They don't pay the bills.

Above: No thanks for the memories
Below: Charlie agrees to help Axel

As Axel feared, Barb wants nothing to do with the plan. She and Hood have a shared, shady past and those unspoken secrets contain more than a few connections as to why Barb came to Steel Harbor in the first place. She kicks them out of the bar without a second thought. After all, her life is complicated and dangerous enough without getting involved in any political crossfire.

Reluctantly, Cora D and Axel mull over their choices. In short, they don't have any. Barb was their one and only hope. No-one else can be trusted. But all is not lost. Barb may have lost her interest in taking up the good fight but her brother, Charlie, still feels a passion for the resistance and follows the couple outside. Finally he has a chance to make a difference again. He secretly agrees to help Axel and Cora D make contact with the resistance. It is a decision he might regret.

Cora D and Axel are introduced to members of one of the resistance headquarters, who are in awe of their legendary leader. For a moment it seems everything is alright, that they can win. But the resistance have bad news. Krebs is dead and the lenses are missing. Schmitz himself has vanished and is probably on the run trying to sell the lenses to the highest bidder. It looks like Axel and Cora D may still need Barb's help.

CORA D: *Axel, I think you're going to have to talk to Barb again.*
AXEL: *Just shoot me now, it'll be easier!*

Better days full of love and rockets!

Back at the Hammerhead, Barb opens a bottle and silently thinks back to her days in Seattle and the time that she and Axel shared in the resistance: fighting all day for the best of causes, making love all night, safe in each other's arms. That had all ended when Axel promised he would go on one last mission. He never came back. He felt his place was there. He sent word to Barb as she was evacuated. Axel's missions continued and Barb left the conflict alone, feeling betrayed by the man she loved. But that is the past and done with forever...or is it?

CHARLIE: *You want some advice?*
BARB: *No.*
CHARLIE: *Drink when you want to remember, Barb. Don't drink when you want to forget.*

Schmitz turns up at the Hammerhead. He realises the complicated power-struggle he has found himself in and will trade the lenses, worth millions of dollars, to Barb in return for her many contacts arranging his safe passage. Barb is tempted but Schmitz pushes the deal a little too hard. He tries to use Charlie, and the chance of restoring his sight, as a bargaining chip. That's a little too close to home and Barb tells him to leave. Schmitz does so, but not before secretly hiding the lenses in the bar. The lenses are too 'hot' to carry around. He hides them where they can be retrieved later. Both Barb and Schmitz are unaware that Charlie, though blind, has heard everything. His

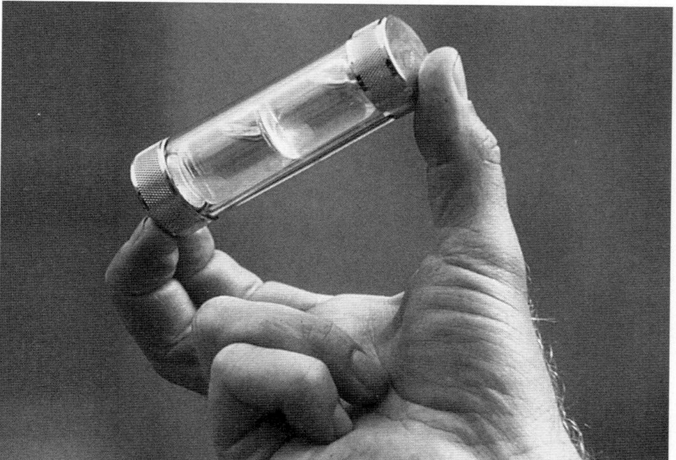

acute hearing is one of his greatest assets. He can pick up sounds that no-one else notices...including where Schmitz hid the box containing the lenses!

Meanwhile Pryzer has used his many torture tools to extract information from one of Schmitz's goons. The fact that the goon is dead doesn't deter Pryzer. His mind-tools allow him to extract information from the lifeless head. Barb Wire features prominently in the dead goon's mind. But then he is a man, so that's perfectly natural! Willis thinks it's nothing more than a fantasy. Pryzer decides to take no chances. He orders the corrupt but reluctant Willis to return to Barb's place and search the Hammerhead for evidence.

Meanwhile, it's becoming obvious that a girl can't even take a few minutes out to clean herself up. Barb is enjoying a few relaxing moments in her luxurious bath above the club. The suds can't wash away all the dirt that clings to the inhabitants of Steel Harbor, but they can provide a break. Suddenly, Barb's relaxation is disturbed by two visitors at the window.

Luckily Barb realises who it is before she shoots them. However she's not so sure she shouldn't shoot them anyway! Cora D and Axel are back. Dressing in front of them (which causes even Axel to go red, and Cora to go a decidedly envious shade of green), Barb

Top and left: Schmitz tries to trade the lenses
Below: Barb cleans up

Above: Uninvited guests
Below: No man is an island, but Fatso gets close

again refuses to help. It would mean way too much trouble if she got caught. Besides, she reasons, she owes Axel nothing. She is even less inclined to help the couple when she discovers that Cora D is actually Axel's wife!

Pryzer turns up at the bar and his goons soon start to cause one hell of a mess. Willis makes a silent apology to Barb. He knows her apolitical stance, but he has little control now that Pryzer has taken command. Quick thinking and a little help from Charlie's vandalism of a retinal scanner lets Axel and Cora D escape from the bar without too much trouble. When the bar is once more empty of visitors, Charlie lifts his dark shades to reveal the retinal lenses, blue against his own useless eyes. No-one thought to check a blind man's eyes for the missing items. Charlie wants to get them to the resistance, Barb sees them as their ticket away from the hell-hole of Steel Harbor. Perhaps Schmitz had a point after all.

Barb goes to see one of the sleaziest big-shots around. The man in question is so obese that he cannot raise himself from the seat he occupies in his own junkyard fortress. His name is, fittingly, Big

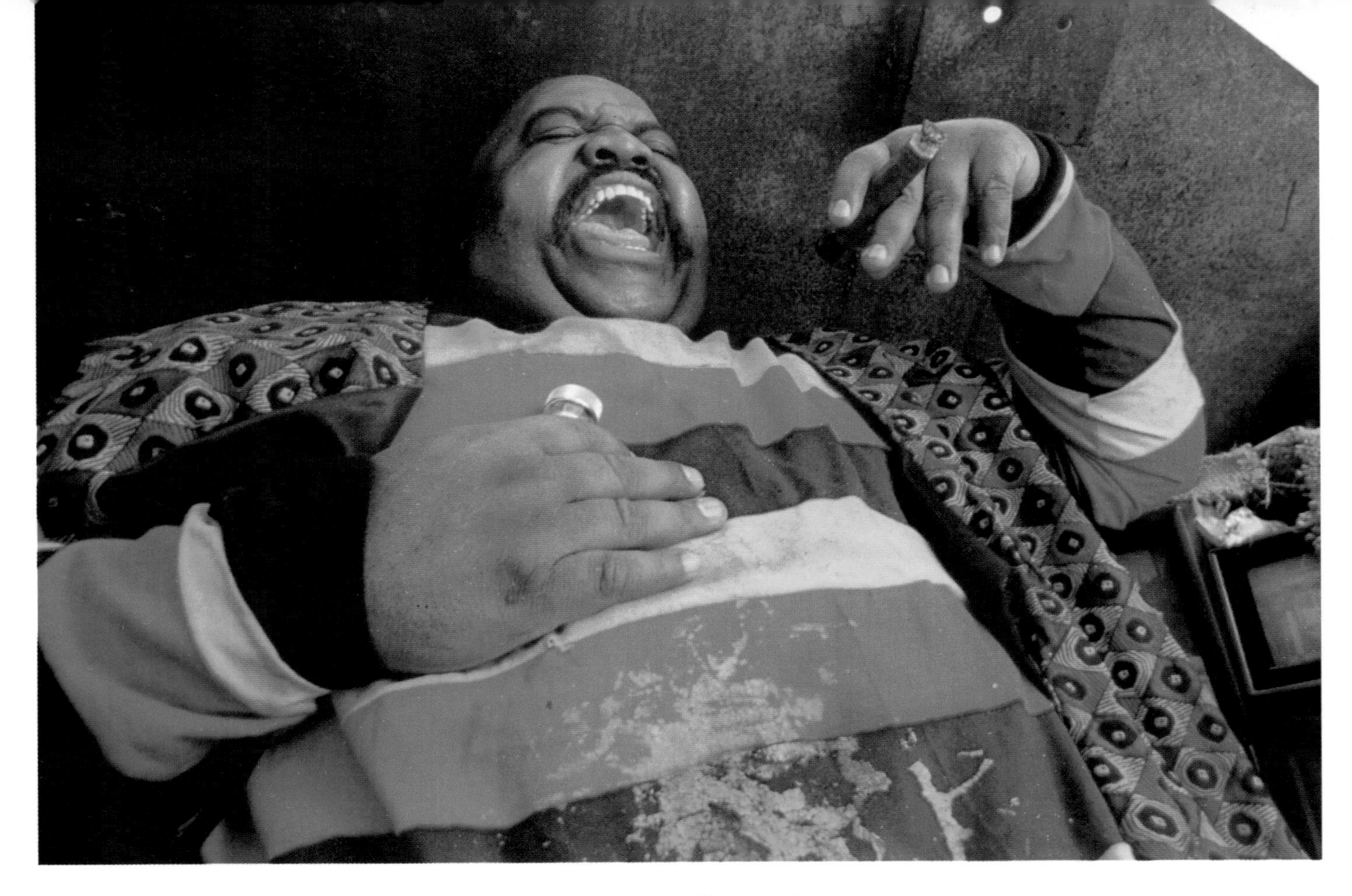

Fatso. Barb is willing to make a deal with Big Fatso – in return for safe passage and a sizeable monetary sum. After heated 'negotiation', a deal is struck.

BIG FATSO: *I have a sudden taste for BARBeque.*

You are what you eat...

Charlie, determined to help the resistance, makes his way to the resistance headquarters he introduced Cora D and Axel to earlier. He is captured by Pryzer, who tortures him, but the Colonel is unable to break the boy's spirit. Instead Pryzer just breaks his body.

Barb guesses what Charlie has done and races to the resistance hide-out. Cora D and Axel have also heard about Pryzer and arrive a few minutes later. A few minutes too late.

Barb finds Charlie has been murdered by the Congressionalists. She can no longer remain neutral. Burying her ill feelings for Axel as deep as she can, she agrees to help Hood and Cora D escape. With the biggest contraband arsenal they can manage, the trio set off in a converted, heavily-armoured bread truck on an adventure which may well decide the fate of the war and world peace itself. Barb is prepared to kill anyone who gets in her way...and heaven help them if they call her 'Babe'!

AXEL: *Does the word 'overkill' mean anything to you?*
BARB: *You ever try to drive out of Steel Harbor?*
AXEL: *No.*
BARB: *Then shut up.*

Big Fatso's deal included safe passage through the various check-points on the way out of Steel Harbor. The kingpin meets her at the first point and, to the horror of Axel and Cora D, Barb proceeds to hand over the lenses. Has she sold them out for her last chance to get out of Steel Harbor? Big Fatso apologises that the 'cash' isn't there but hands her a credit card equivalent.

Naturally, it's all a trap. Big Fatso opens a refrigerator; inside Schmitz's dead body is being kept on ice. Suddenly Pryzer and his goons appear. It seems like Pryzer and Big Fatso have won. Pryzer will have his lenses, the resistance will lose its most enigmatic leader and the secrets of the Directorate's plans will remain intact. Big Fatso will also be rich beyond his dreams. Pryzer instructs Willis to handcuff Barb, Cora D and Axel. Secretly (and rather surprisingly) Willis only pretends to cuff the prisoners and slips Barb a grenade.

Above and below: You never know who you can trust...

A few seconds later, all hell breaks loose. Barb throws the grenade high into the air and opens fire on Pryzer and his goons. As Barb and her allies head for their vehicle, the grenade falls from the sky and lands in the lap of the immobile Big Fatso. Suddenly bits of Fatso become extremely mobile in every conceivable direction.

WILLIS: *How'd I do, Barb?*
BARB: *Willis, you're the last person I ever expected to come through in a pinch.*
WILLIS: *I can't believe it myself!*

Willis joins them on the bread van as they make their escape. Pryzer and his troops are in hot pursuit and a fire-fight ensues. The bread van is heavily armoured but it won't stand up for long against the Directorate's weapons. In a mirror image of the events years before, it's now Barb who stays behind

to help the others escape – roaring back towards Pryzer's troops on her motorbike and providing the fugitives with a few extra seconds. She manages to take out one of the pursuing vehicles as they hurtle into a warehouse yard.

The bread van is finally knocked from the road, but Barb ensures that Pryzer is too preoccupied with her to follow the rest of them. She thinks she has fatally wounded the Colonel, but he emerges from the shadows in a monster-sized fork-lift truck aimed right for Barb. The fork-lift's prongs hook into Barb's bike and she's soon holding on for dear life as the

Above: I'll be back?
Right: A congressional soldier takes a long walk off a short crane

truck smashes into more and more cars and vehicles. When it finally comes to rest, Pryzer stands defiantly, his gun firmly pointing at Barb. It seems it is all over.

But both Pryzer and Barb have momentarily forgotten about Axel. Apparently from nowhere, a huge hook descends and attaches itself to the fork-lift. Axel is now controlling the warehouse's huge crane and proceeds to lift the truck further and further from the ground below.

It's now one-on-one as Barb and Pryzer go head to head in the final conflict. Barb is an expert in hand-to-hand combat, but Pryzer is stronger. She knows that time is running out. Pryzer is winning, Barb is unable to escape his attack. Pryzer begins to gloat.

PRYZER: *This is just like my favourite song...I got you, BABE!*
BARB: *Don't call me 'Babe'!*

Now that got Barb really angry. With one final kick she leaps for the crane's hook as Axel releases the fork-lift. For a second everything is frozen in time, then Pryzer and the vehicle plunge to destruction: a fitting end to a villain who had the nerve to refer to Barb that way. No-one calls her 'Babe'!

Barb, Cora D, Axel and Willis have survived – but what about the retinal contact lenses? Look deeply into Barb's eyes for the answer. She has been wearing them. Charlie wasn't the only person who could improvise. Now Cora D can make it safely through the airport check-point, to her plane and on to Canada.

Above: Escape to victory
Below: The long goodbye

BARB: *Why'd you come back?*
AXEL: *I couldn't leave you twice.*

Axel and Barb share one last passionate kiss. Axel wonders whether he should stay. But he has another life now – not to mention a wife who might object! Axel and Barb have had their time together, now it's time to move on. Some of those bridges between them are now rebuilt and Barb bids him farewell. A few moments later, the plane takes off with perhaps mankind's last hope.

Barb and Willis head back towards Steel Harbor. Willis comments that Barb hasn't come away from the mission with anything. She disagrees...and produces the gold credit card that Big Fatso had no time to retrieve. It's her ticket out of Steel Harbor – to Paris, perhaps?

WILLIS: *Want some company?*
BARB: *No. Goodbye, Willis.*
WILLIS: *Too bad. I do believe I'm falling in love.*
BARB: *Get in line.*

Barb rides out across a sunlit landscape on her motorcycle, blonde hair streaming in the wind. She races forward into the future...

FADE TO BLACK.

Chapter 2

CAST AND CHARACTERS

Time to take a look at the actors you'll see in *Barb Wire* and their own views on the characters they portray and the events they find themselves in. Starting with...

PAMELA ANDERSON as Barb Wire

Pamela Anderson was the obvious choice to play Barb Wire. One look at the character in the comic book and the similarities are clear to see. Pamela may not go around toting guns, but her looks, her fitness and her high television profile made her the leading contender for the role.

Pamela was born on Vancouver Island and later moved to Vancouver City. Her first step on the road to stardom was in fact a strange twist of fate. She was attending a British Columbia Lions football game when the camera picked her out of the crowd and displayed her image on the stadium's giant screen. The fans cheered and she was brought down to the 50-yard line, where she was introduced to the appreciative crowd. She was wearing a Labatt's Beer T-shirt and the company realised they had quite an opportunity on their hands. Pamela was immediately signed up to the company. She became their 'Blue Zone' girl. That campaign proved so successful that other promotions and advertisements followed soon after.

A billboard image of Pamela brought her to the attention of the magazine *Playboy* and she subsequently moved to Los Angeles. Television work came next and she was a regular recurring character (The Tool-Time Girl) on the hit ABC Television series *Home Improvement* starring comedian Tim Allen, which has now been very successful on British television and around the world.

At the same time Pamela was also working on another hit programme. The name of the show? Where have you been recently? It is, of course, *Baywatch*, often referred to as the most popular family drama on television. The show is now seen on every continent on the planet (apparently even the snowy wastes of Antarctica have been warmed by various settlements requesting the chance to see the sunny show) and has a combined viewing audience of over one billion in more than 110 countries. Not bad for a show that was once threatened with the axe, but roared back to success with the aid of its fans in both Europe and America. Anderson's *Baywatch* character is C.J. Parker, one of the dedicated Los Angeles County Lifeguards ready to hurl themselves into the surf to save anyone in trouble – and that's only when they don't have some personal problem, moral dilemma or conspiracy to sort out. Due to the phenomenal success of the show, Pamela decided to hang up her Tool-Time belt on *Home Improvement* and concentrate on working full time with *Baywatch*. She hasn't looked back since.

She made her feature film debut in the movie *Snapdragon*, an erotic thriller, opposite actor Steven Bauer. This was followed by the action comedy *Good Cop, Bad Cop*, in which she starred opposite Robert Hayes and David Keith. Pamela recently filmed a CBS

'Movie of the Week' entitled *Deader Than Ever*, an updated Mike Hammer mystery. That was followed by a television pilot called *Eden Quest*, a programme which goes behind the scenes with men and women who indulge in extreme high adrenaline sports and high profile professions. The idea was so successful that there have been several more installments and more planned for the future.

Barb Wire provides Anderson with an opportunity to play a less 'sweet' role than that of C.J. Parker:

"She's not sugar and spice [like C.J.]. Yeah, it's very different from *Baywatch*. C.J. is very happy, sweet and kinda apple-pie. Barb blows away baddies without any remorse. I've always wanted a part than involves kicking ass. Barb's a psychotic, bitter woman." [Pamela laughs.] "I guess she does have that twisted little streak inside of her head. She kinda plays everybody and works everybody for everything that she gets. When Axel left her, she came to the depths of the worst part of town.

"I think that Barb is probably closer to the real me. This is the best role, the best showcase that I could ever do. I've always been athletic, I took kick-boxing lessons and some karate. The kick-boxing is unbelievable, I want to continue with it. I've done a lot of my own stunts *and* while wearing a corset that fits my waist in seventeen inches. Every time I turned around, I was more scared of falling out of my costume than anything else!

"It's great to play a character like Barb. She's definitely in control, everyone listens to her, she does what she wants. She gets what she wants by using everything she has. She always has a different scheme, she acts differently with everybody. But she's very independent.

"The only person she really cares about is her brother. Charlie (or rather Jack Noseworthy) looks exactly like my brother in real life. I've a picture of Jack, my brother and me together and they look so similar. I was instantly protective of Jack. Charlie has that attitude, you know how younger brothers always seem to know everything and be very philosophical!"

In 1995 she married rock star Tommy Lee and changed her professional name to Pamela Lee. Even the Motley Crue member has a part to play in the movie: the soundtrack. "Tommy, my husband, is going to be doing some of the music for the movie – not with Motley Crue this time, just by himself."

TEMEURA MORRISON as Axel Hood

The role of Axel Hood required an actor with a 'tough' look and imposing screen presence. Temeura Morrison possesses those qualities in abundance.

Born in Rotorua, New Zealand, and based in Auckland, he has gained a strong reputation as a film and television actor. Internationally, he is probably best known for the critically acclaimed *Once Were Warriors*, a tale of contemporary Maori life which received praise across the world for its compelling performances and graphic, hard-hitting story.

"We try to make the characters (in *Barb Wire*) interesting. I don't play too far away from myself. The producers saw me in *Once Were Warriors* and they wanted me, as I understand,

from that performance. I looked at what I did there and saw a certain amount of physical strength and presence, so I just tried to use those qualities.

"Axel is a freedom fighter for the resistance. He met with Barb in an 'earlier' life and subsequently they were supposed to meet, go away together and live happily ever after. But Axel got called away on other resistance missions and ended up with Cora D, the woman who has discovered some bad things about the powers-that-be. As a result of circumstances, Axel crosses paths with Barb again..."

It's not all wham, bang, kick, thrust and mutilate, though. Temeura has made sure that Axel is a fully rounded character.

"When you get to the lighter scenes, I tried to give it a softer touch...so you're not *always* hard and aggressive, physical and onto it all the time. That gives the character a bit of colour. You work from the script. The script gives you the background. Axel's background is a man who's lived on guts, muscle and luck...that about sums it up. You use your imagination and trust the director! When they call 'Action!' you work off your instincts and you throw something in. The director will bring it up a bit, take it down a bit, fine tune it.

"It's a good fantasy tale, but the big thing is having the woman as the hero. She's like a Mad Max, road warrior character."

Temeura also relished the chance to work with a strong group of actors.

"For me, as an actor, it's been very rewarding to see people like Steve Railsback [Pryzer] who was amazing in *Helter Skelter* [as Charles Manson] and, of course, *The Stuntsman* [with Peter O'Toole]. They may not have had the breaks like, say, Tommy Lee Jones, but they are very fine actors who have come from a real professional hard-work-based foundation. I've been watching what they do, I learn from everybody."

Temeura's previous movies have included John Laing's *Other Halves*, Geoff Murphy's *Never Say Die* and Merata Mita's *Mauri*. He also worked as an adviser on the Oscar-winning and internationally successful *The Piano*, directed by Jane Campion.

On television he appeared in the top-rating New Zealand drama series *Shortland Street* in which he starred as the laid-back Dr Hone Ropata (a totally different type of character to the role of Jake in *Once Were Warriors* which he began a few days after leaving the set of the TV series) as well as *Seekers*, *Shark in the Park*, *Adventurers* and *Gold*.

VICTORIA ROWELL as Cora D

In casting the role of Doctor Corrina Devonshire (otherwise known as Cora D, the leader of the resistance), the film-makers needed a strong and capable actress. Victoria Rowell has already had a successful career in both film and television. She starred as Amanda Bentley in the CBS series *Diagnosis: Murder* and as

Drucilla Barber-Winters in the American number-one-rated daytime drama *The Young and the Restless*. She guested on *One Life to Live* and *As the World Turns*. Victoria also appeared in the TV movies *Secret Sins of the Father*, *The Pack* and *The Last Set*. She also had recurring parts in the top-rated *The Cosby Show*, *The Fresh Prince of Bel Air* and *Herman's Head*.

Over the last few years she has appeared in many successful big screen movies. She starred opposite Eddie Murphy in the film *The Distinguished Gentlemen* and was reunited with Bill Cosby in the comedy *Leonard: Part 6*. Her most recent big screen appearance was in Jim (*The Mask*) Carrey's hit movie *Dumb and Dumber*. Victoria admits:

> "Cora is a fugitive for most of this movie. She's got involved with chemical warfare. That's really *not* what her intention was, but that's what she became involved in. She absconds with the information on the weapon and is being sought after by the bad guys."

Cora D finds herself none too keen on the voluptuous Barb, though she needs her to keep one step ahead of Pryzer, and lucky Axel finds himself in a romantic triangle with two attractive women.

> "Given that I'm in khaki overalls the entire time and Pamela's in the leather, she really does give me a run for my money! But you'll have to see the movie to see what happens, I haven't given up!"

The encounter at the Hammerhead is the first time that the two women in Axel's life have met. Needless to say, Axel hasn't spoken about Barb too much and Barb herself doesn't know what has happened in the intervening years. When they finally meet up, "Cora D is pissed! She didn't quite understand what the relationship was between these two people and Axel wasn't being very clear. Cora doesn't have an axe to grind with Axel [sic] because his affair with Barb was before their marriage, but she knows that there's something lingering there!"

STEVE RAILSBACK as Colonel Victor Pryzer

Picked to play the evil, manipulating, sadistic and generally bad Colonel Pryzer is character actor Steve Railsback. A native of Dallas, Texas, Railsback moved to New York and studied for a career in acting under

the renowned Lee Strasberg. He appeared in many off-Broadway shows including *Little Foxes* and *The Cherry Orchard*.

He received high praise for the role of Charles Manson in the controversial 1976 television mini-series *Helter Skelter*. His other movies include *The Stuntsman*, *Calendar Girl* and *Armed & Dangerous*. On television he has appeared in top-rated shows such as *The X-Files* (in which he played the pivotal character of Duane Barry).

JACK NOSEWORTHY as Charlie Kopetski

Before taking the part of Barb's passionate and gutsy younger brother, Jack Noseworthy starred in several box office successes including *S.F.W.*, *Alive* and the comedy *Encino Man*. He also took the role of Eric in the hit movie *The Brady Bunch*.

On television he took the starring role in MTV's first original drama series *Dead at 21* and was a regular on the comedy *Teech*. He is also an accomplished singer and dancer and has appeared in productions of *Cats*, *A Chorus Line* and *Equus* for which he received a Los Angeles Drama Critics' Circle Award and a Dramalogue Award for Best Actor.

"I think Barb and Charlie's relationship is the single most important relationship in her life and in 'mine'. Charlie relies on her so much. It's taken Charlie a long time to realise that he relies on her as much as he does. You see that they really care about each other. Whatever type of movie it is, you have to see people connect.

"Charlie and Barb were resistance fighters. In the course of fighting this civil war in the United States, Charlie was blinded by a grenade. Barb's now opened the Hammerhead Bar and given up fighting for the resistance. Her passion for it has gone, but Charlie's is still there. Poor Charlie, he can't do what he wants to do, he can't fight in the resistance, he's turned to drink a bit. But he isn't able to do anything for the resistance because he's blind.

"My character discovers a way to help the resistance and fight for what he thinks is right. He discovers a way to work for them without Barb knowing. She doesn't want to be involved, but Charlie does. I find that I *can* work and make things happen by *being* blind and *without* the assistance of Barb.

"When I read the comic books, I didn't really connect to it as much. But that was good, because when I let go of the comic book and read the script, the character was fully fleshed out. I didn't really base my character on the comic book, I based it on the script.

"My first day was like being G.I. Joe because it was the flashback sequence. I'm working for the resistance and I still have my sight. I was running through fire and shooting guns and throwing grenades. I was in a helicopter, lifting off the ground and pulling Pamela in. It was the coolest thing. I never want to do anything other than action adventure movies because they are just so much fun! It's like every guy's dream...to run around and take care of Pamela Anderson!"

XANDER BERKELEY as Alexander Willis

Starring as the morally dubious Alexander Willis, Chief of Police, is yet another interesting part for Xander Berkeley, an actor who has appeared in many blockbusting movies for an equally impressive list of directors. He has starred in films such as Ron Howard's *Apollo 13*, Rob Reiner's *A Few Good Men*, James Cameron's *Terminator 2*, Mike Figgis's *Leaving Las Vegas* and *Internal Affairs* and Clint Eastwood's *The Rookie*. His most recent movie is the critically acclaimed *Heat* with Robert De Niro and Al Pacino.

His TV credits include roles on *New York Undercover*, the CBS series *Donato and Daughter* and the NBC mini-series *Deadly Matrimony*. He also

starred in the Showtime original film *Roswell* and the HBO film *Attack of the 50ft Woman*.

Berkeley enjoys playing Willis, the one person who's technically as neutral as Barb – in the sense that he's willing to be bribed by either side:

"He's the corrupt Chief of Police, with a heart of gold as it turns out, although his mind is preoccupied with gold and money constantly throughout the whole movie. That's his *modus operandi*. You can't tell whether he's on this side or that side, basically he's on the take and out for himself. But he does save the day in the end!"

Barb and Willis may not see eye to eye, but they have common ground and find themselves going after the same things for different reasons.

"There are certain echoes in the relationship between Barb and Willis, that existed in between Humphrey Bogart and Claude Rains's characters in *Casablanca*. It's the beginning of a beautiful friendship throughout, but they are pitted against one another. Once Pryzer comes in, eventually Barb and Willis become united against a common enemy."

Willis, usually the only form of law and order (or what passes for it) in Steel Harbor, is small potatoes compared to the threat of the nasty Colonel Pryzer who usurps Willis's authority. "I think there's a certain bemused attachment to Willis that prevents him from ever feeling his powers being taken away. He has a sense of humour and Pryzer doesn't. He doesn't have to take Pryzer all that seriously, as long as he doesn't get himself killed."

The fact that Barb is originally a comic book character makes the whole movie much more fun, Berkeley admits. "There's something fun and liberating about the fact that it's taken from a comic book. There's different homages in the film to film noir in the writing where it's really snappy. It's a different reality, it keeps the sense of humour going and keeps the thing alive when you come out of an action sequence."

UDO KIER as Curly

The renowned European actor Udo Kier takes the role of Barb's (follically-challenged) head waiter at the Hammerhead, making sure that everything runs smoothly, or at least that nothing expensive gets broken.

In the early 1970s Kier took the roles of Dracula and Frankenstein in two of Andy Warhol's seminal movies. He then collaborated (over a fifteen-year period) with German avant-garde film director Rainer Fassbinder, taking leads in films such as *The Third Generation*. He also starred in the film *Zentropa* which garnered the Jury Prize for Best Technical Film at the 1992 Cannes Film Festival.

His American film credits include the highly successful *Ace Ventura: Pet Detective* opposite Jim Carrey, Gus Van Sant's *My Own Private Idaho* and the recent *Johnny Mnemonic* with Keanu Reeves.

ROSEY BROWN as Big Fatso

Taking the role of Big Fatso, the kingpin of crime (and generally disgusting and sleazy things) in Steel Harbor is actor Rosey Brown. While working in the Seattle police force, Brown was approached by a director who encouraged him to move to Los Angeles to pursue his acting career. Brown now works extensively in television and film and is still employed by the LA police force.

His TV credits include *Fresh Prince of Bel Air, In Living Color* and *The Golden Girls*. He has also appeared in such box-office successes as *Tango and Cash* with Sylvester Stallone and Kurt Russell, *Throw Momma From The Train* with Danny DeVito and Billy Crystal as well as the upcoming features *Space Jam* with Michael Jordan and *King Pin* starring Woody Harrelson.

Chapter 3

BARB WIRE: THE COMIC

Success at a gallop

Before the film of *Barb Wire* was a mere twinkle in the eyes of Hollywood, the character was already carving herself a legend within the pages of her own comic book. In the following pages, we take a look at the success story of Dark Horse Comics and Barb Wire.

Mike Richardson is the founder of Dark Horse Comics and the President of Dark Horse Entertainment, the sister-company recently created to deal with the cinematic possibilities of Dark Horse characters. He created the publishing house after hearing several comic book artists bemoan the fact that most of the dominant comic book publishers did not allow any artistic control of the characters created by their employees. Richardson realised that this, combined with an industry screaming for new concepts, would allow an independent publisher to enter the industry and attract both talent and attention, if handled and promoted well. He founded Dark Horse in 1986 with editor Randy Stradley (and later, business consultant Neil Hankerson). As he'd hoped, the working conditions attracted some of the comic industry's top talent. Richardson hoped to sell 10,000 copies of his first publication, *Dark Horse Presents*. When sales passed 50,000 he knew he was on to a winner.

Many respected artists and writers have produced work for the company, including Frank Miller (who had already reinvented DC's *Batman* for a whole new audience), Dave Gibbons (the artist on DC's other milestone series, *Watchmen*), John Byrne (who at one time or another has drawn just about every superhero going) Archie Goodwin, Al Williamson, Mike Allred, John Wagner and science-fiction veteran Harlan Ellison.

Out of a field of more than 150 US-based book publishers, Dark Horse has built on early successes and now ranks fourth. Its output ranges from monthly comic books to graphic novels, Manga reprints and its own superhero universe in which Barb Wire, despite having no special powers, is a major player.

Barb Wire is the creation of writer/artist Chris Warner and first saw print as part of a 16-issue limited series called *Comics' Greatest World* from Dark Horse Comics. But the basic idea of the character began to form over a decade ago.

Chris had worked in the music business, doing illustrations for record stores and local bands. He had also worked at a speciality publishing house that was doing a lot of speech rehabilitation work. He got into comics when he tired of the eight-to-five work routine:

> "I broke into comics quite late. Most guys seem to break into the industry in their early twenties. I was nearly thirty. I took an inventory of my skills and realised that comics was all I was capable of doing. Once I broke in, I wanted to write as well.

"In 1986 I conceived Barb Wire, a character that was a little different than the current version, but a woman who was still a lot of fun, very feisty, lots of action. I kicked the idea around for several years and never really did much with it.

"When Dark Horse decided to develop their own superhero universe, Barb was one of the characters that Mike was interested in. At the time, I didn't think that I would have any time to develop the character on my own, so I agreed to sell the character to Dark Horse and develop it with them. She got introduced in the *Comics' Greatest World* and now she's in the movies!"

Somewhat surprisingly, Warner – a talented and established artist – chose only to write the *Comics' Greatest World* instalment of his character and decided not to carry out the artistic chores as well. When the character was launched in her own comics series Warner allowed other writers to build on his original concept.

"There were other things I wanted to work on. Part of the idea of developing and selling a concept to someone is to have other people to work on it. If you're going to do all the work yourself, you might as well keep it as a creator-owned project. I developed a character called Black Cross several years ago, and I still own it. With Barb Wire and some of the other characters I created (including Pit-Bulls and Motorhead), I knew that if I didn't get the characters and ideas out there, the comics industry being what it is, someone else would come up with similar ideas. I still had heavy input into the characters and, contractually, I can come back and work on them if I want in the future. I have the best of both worlds!"

The comic version, as mentioned, was part of a linked series of titles with a superhero theme and though Barb had no powers (with the possible exception of being able to escape hypothermia while wearing incredibly skimpy outfits!) she was often asked to bring in bail-jumpers who possessed super-human abilities. The flip-side was that Barb got paid the big bucks because her targets were so dangerous. Naturally the superhero angle has been played down for the movie, with more attention paid to the politics that Barb encounters – and deals with in her own sweet way.

"Even though the film changes some of the elements from the comic (they've left out the other related superheroes to make Barb Wire work better) I think the character and the environment is very consistent with the comic. The original concept of Steel Harbor was more of a science-fiction, cyberpunk scenario set in the future. I was going to call it Metal City, but it was a little close to *Sin City* by Frank [Miller, the man behind DC's *The Dark Knight Returns*] so we changed it to Steel Harbor. So I had this environment in mind for Barb and a few other characters that I'd created. It was a decayed, industrial urban environment, which I thought Barb fit into quite well."

Barb's catchphrase *Don't call me 'Babe'* is bound to catch on but Chris admits that, at first, he didn't like it too much:

"It's funny, I can recall when John Arcudi was writing the first few issues of the first Barb Wire comic series that there were some similar lines to that [actually: 'Don't call me Honey']. *Don't call me 'Babe'* ended up on the cover of the first issue and I hated it. But in the context of the film it works. When you hear Pamela saying it, it really works. So I've incorporated it back into the [post-film] continuity of the comics.

"The catchphrase is tongue-in-cheek. When I actually think about the character and how Barb might relate to some of the women in the audience, then there's something both fun *and* strong about it. It says: you can dress how you want, look the way you want and act the way you want and still have the right to demand respect. That was always a real element of Barb. She dresses how she dresses because *she* wants to. That shouldn't carry any further baggage. You should be able to dress attractively *without*

Cover and panel from Barb's first Dark Horse series

being regarded as an object, or depersonalised or dehumanised. I hope the film will draw more women to the comic.

"Barb is a strong character who runs her own show, does her own thing. She has no agenda, she just does what she wants to, not what is expected by men or women. That's a good role model. Mind you, riding around on motorcycles and chasing criminals might not be. But hey, if I looked like Barb Wire/Pamela Anderson I'd be proud to show myself off!"

Mike Richardson paints a similar picture:

"Barb Wire is a resourceful character, she's the most resourceful character in Steel Harbor. All streets lead to her bar. She has a definite, positive image. Her destiny is in her own hands. She's made in much the same tradition as the strong male lead. It's a role that could very easily be reversed and you'd have a character that could be played by someone like Sylvester Stallone or Arnold Schwarzenegger. Barb Wire is smart, resourceful and she kicks butt!"

No-one who has read the comic books can fail to notice that, visually at least, Barb already had more than a passing resemblance to Pamela Anderson. "Actually Pam was probably about 16 when I came up with the original concept, so Barb wasn't based on her," Chris laughs, but he's more than happy with the choice of actress. "I got the chance to meet Pamela and I did some preliminary costume designs which we looked at together. I had a whole sheaf of photos that I'd torn out of wild fashion mags and we discussed what she liked. Some of the stuff that's used in the movie is a hybrid of those designs and will be

featured in the relaunched comic released shortly after the film's release."

Chris's other projects include working on other Dark Horse series including the *Aliens vs Predator* series, a concept that has been so popular that there is talk in Hollywood of teaming up the monsters in a big-budget movie.

Mike Richardson created the character of The Mask which went on to become a huge international success story when Jim Carrey took the role in the silver screen version. Hundreds of millions of dollars later, a sequel is already in the works. Richardson also created the *Timecop* premise which went on to star Jean-Claude Van Damme.

Given the interest in Dark Horse characters, it was only a matter of time before the likes of Barb Wire and The Mask made the journey to cinema screens. Dark Horse Entertainment was the company formed to look at such options and in just a few years has become a significant player in the Hollywood industry. Currently Dark Horse has a 'first-look' deal with Universal Pictures. Universal is committed to help develop no less than nine projects with Dark Horse over the next three years...and that *doesn't* include a separate agreement Dark Horse made with producer Lawrence Gordon to co-develop eight pictures together.

"We feel our success validates our production philosophy," says Mike. "We strive to impart our creative input to all levels of the production process, rather than simply licensing comic book properties for development by others."

OTHER CHARACTERS

Though you won't see them in the movie (though maybe in a sequel), Barb's supporting cast in the comic have definitely contributed to her success so far. It seems only fair to give them a name-check so we thought a brief rundown was in order:

The Machine: Barb's right hand – well, machine. He used to be a man called Avram Roman, but he is now the victim of a government-imposed self-repair system. Every time it is used, it replaces part of Roman's humanity with artificial components. But one advantage is that, while he's staying at the Hammerhead, he's one impressive line of defence. The character is now being considered for his own movie!

Motorhead: No, not the rock group. Frank Fletcher is the some-time number one bouncer for the Hammerhead. He has the unstable ability to use telekinetic energy which is only slightly less painful for Frank than it is for the unlucky person who gets hit by it. He has tattoos covering most of his body. Oh yes, did we mention he hears voices in his head? Not your everyday citizen of Steel Harbor...or maybe he is!

Faith Perdue: Steel Harbor's leading citizen. She is the heir to a huge industrial fortune and a major mover-and-shaker who wants to return the area to its former glory.

An array of colourful friends and enemies from the pages of Barb Wire

Wolf Gang: The words 'dark alley' and 'wouldn't want to meet' spring to mind. Of the many gangs that run riot in Steel Harbor, Wolf Gang has the unique distinction of being fully supported by the city's government in combating the exploitation and extortion practised by other gangs. Sounds a little like letting the fox watch the hen-house. Its members include unruly thugs with names such as Hunter, Bomber, Burner, Breaker and Cutter – but these are a lot tougher than any Gladiator!

Mace Blitzkrieg: A big, hairy, one-man wrecking crew who's carved out the city's largest gang turf with his fists – making him the baddest villain in Steel Harbor. His crew, the Prime Movers, includes Airborne, a super-soldier capable of flight and armed to the teeth; Deadlight, a woman who can drain the life from any living thing; Killerwatt, who generates electrical energy; and Blackbelt, a martial arts pro who can kick her way through solid steel. You don't want to get on the wrong side of these guys!

Chapter 4

NEXT STOP: HOLLYWOOD

It's tempting to think that getting any film made is easy. Audiences only see the finished result. In reality, film-making is anything but easy.

Anyone who has seen a film or TV show being made should realise that there is a great deal of time spent on getting everything right. Murphy's Law states that anything that can go wrong will go wrong and never is that more true than on a feature film. From noise off-camera to finance, from scheduling to illness – all are problems that frequently need to be overcome. *Barb Wire* was no exception to the rule. Here we take a look at how the film got made and talk to the people who overcame the many obstacles along the way.

Early Days

It's always a big step translating a character from the printed page to the silver screen. Each medium has it's own distinctive advantages and feel. Bringing Barb Wire to cinemas involved careful planning and decision making. Who would the film star? Who could write a good enough script? Who would take the directing chores? That's not even taking into account distribution deals and marketing. Mike Richardson agrees that Dark Horse's growing success helped get the ball rolling. "The success of *The Mask* helped a lot. During the summer that *The Mask* was released, the number one and number three movies in the United States were characters I had created. *Timecop* was the other film. Those successes certainly helped my and Dark Horse's credibility."

So a first step was taken and interest was sparked, but many films enter pre-production and only a handful eventually find their way to the nearest multiplex. Decisions needed to be made, and wrong decisions could mean the difference between success and failure.

For instance: it's the cast that the public first notice and a capable actress with the right credentials, look and ability to play Barb Wire was needed to be the figurehead of the project and film. There was one obvious choice.

"When we first discussed doing the film with Larry Gordon at Universal, Pamela's name came up because one of the producers, Brad Weyman, knew her manager. He had looked at the cover of one of the Barb Wire comics and commented that it looked like Pamela Anderson. He said we had to meet her and so we did. We immediately thought she was perfect for the role. She looked the part perfectly, she is physically right and can move very well. We thought the role was made for her. She felt the same way."

"My manager said I shouldn't do it, but I said 'well, let me see it'," explains Pamela. "I looked at it and thought 'Absolutely. This is totally me!'"

"She'd always wanted to do an action film and – she coined the phrase – she'd always wanted to be Pambo!" Mike Richardson laughs. "I think it was late 1994 when we talked to PolyGram and said let's make *Barb Wire*. We told them that we already had Pamela. They were very excited and said let's go with it. We started shooting on May 23rd 1995 for an eight/nine

Steel Harbor welcomes careful drivers...

week filming period, about average length for that type of movie."

Though that was the case, the shoot wasn't to go too smoothly – but more of that shortly. Nowadays simply having a star is no cast-iron guarantee of great box-office. Both Stallone and Schwarzenegger have had flops. What's also needed is a good story for the actor to work with and that, Richardson explains, is what Dark Horse do best:

"What we tried to do was concentrate very hard on getting a solid story. The character seems to fall into place if the story is there. That's our focus. Comics are much different than motion pictures. They have different means of developing characters. There are things you can take for granted in the comics that you can't take for granted in films. You need a tight, cohesive story. One thing that we make sure of is tight consistency of logic in our stories but with some nice twists and turns. So many movies today miss that. The logic seems to go out of the window in some scenes. We focus on story. Our comic books are story-driven rather than character-driven anyway. That makes our properties easier to translate from page to screen."

"The unique thing in Dark Horse is that we know our stories, we've lived and nurtured them." explains producer Todd Moyer. "We're not going to watch other people dissect and interpret them; we remain in charge of the creative vision behind our projects."

"Chuck Pfarrer wrote the script. He's a very talented writer. He's also done a number of movies, such as a Jean-Claude Van Damme movie [*Hard Target*] and *Navy Seals*, so he really knows how to handle action. He's already working on one of our next film projects, *Virus*," Richardson adds.

Deadly Designs

Even when a script and stars have been found, the process of film-making is still far from beginning, never mind being complete. Each film, whether it be *Barb Wire* or a period piece (such as, say, *Age of Innocence* or *Howard's End*), requires experts to dress the characters and set properly, to come up with designs that suit and reflect the 'feel' of the film and its environment. For *Barb Wire* there was a lot more scope for experimenting. After all, the future is a great playground.

Production Designer, Jean-Philippe Carp, is one of the senior members of the production team to whom that task falls. "I was brought onto the project by Tim Clawson from Propaganda and Todd Moyer from Dark Horse," Jean-Philippe explains.

"They chose me because I was the Production Designer on a French film *Delicatessen* for which I received the French Academy Award (the 'César') in 1992 and for *Johnny Mnemonic*, the interactive game produced by Propaganda.

"I started working and thinking about *Barb Wire* in February 1995. My first drawings, on computer, which you could walk through, came around the middle of March. Part of all our jobs is to communicate our vision – mine as a Production Designer. The directors need to feel comfortable in the space I conceive. I didn't have any specific problems. None of the sets that I proposed were denied. The producers gave me a blank card because they trusted me. Maybe the biggest problems were the usual: time and money!"

The bar area was designed to be heavily armoured

He admits that creating Barb's world (and specifically the Hammerhead Bar) is a mixture of looking at the comic, scrutinizing the script and using a lot of imagination.

"I stuck in my mind the sensitive impressions received from the comic book. Step by step, the character became more and more clear. I understood better and better what was hidden between the lines. The context of the script itself was indicating the necessary transposition. Remember that it takes place after a kind of civil war. Part of Steel Harbor is destroyed. People are tough. Most of them live on the streets. The winners have money and go and spend it in the only bar where they may make business too. Everyone has a weapon to protect themselves. Fight or murder are the only two languages spoken. That's why the bar is mostly metal, bartenders protected from customers by chain link and barbed wires.

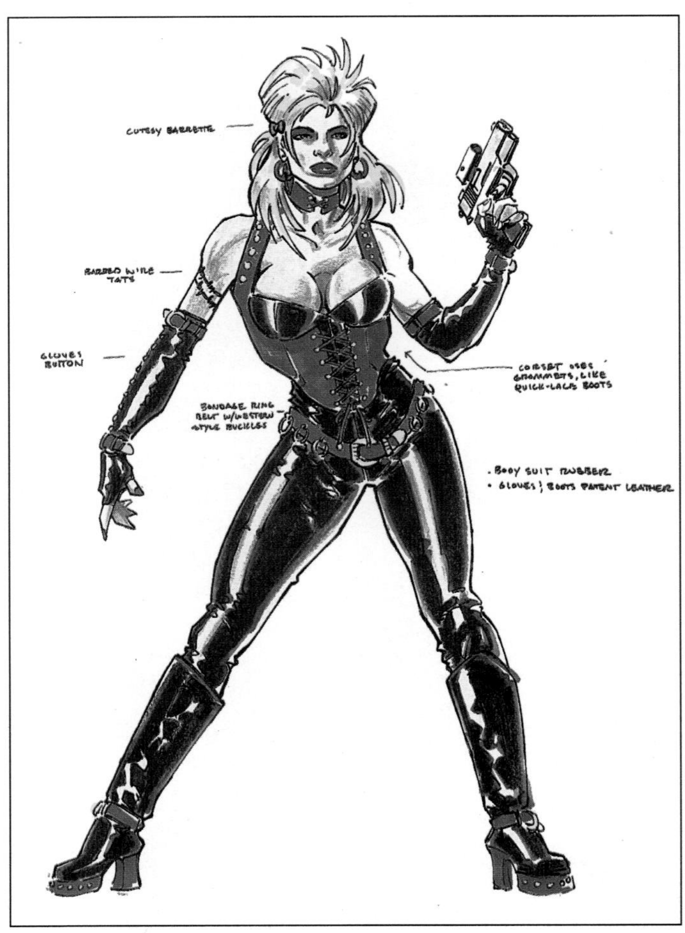

"The place itself is an abandoned hardware store with a broken ceiling, adapted as platforms to have an overview of the audience. A specific one is used by the band. The DJ booth hangs on the wall. The challenge was to use the hardware store and take advantage of its own configuration. The logic came from the script and the space of the location."

Rosanna Norton is the Costume Designer on *Barb Wire*, chosen from many possible candidates because of her extensive experience within the industry. Rosanna was Oscar-nominated for her work on the ground-breaking *TRON* and has since designed the look of may other successful films such as *Innerspace*, *The Flintstones*, *The Brady Bunch* and its sequel.

"*Barb Wire* is quite like *TRON* in the sense that this is a 'fantasy' movie which I really, really enjoy doing. You can go far out and to extremes, it's in another world. I do like doing comic book stuff. Todd Moyer hired me [for *Barb Wire*] back in February 1995. We just jumped in and started working. We put together sketches and ideas. They let me do pretty much what I wanted. For the people in the Hammerhead club we did a lot of skimpy costumes, lots of leather and chains."

Obviously some changes were made in transferring Barb to the big screen.

"Barb doesn't look quite like she does in the comic. We decided on black for her. In the comic she wears blue and pink which is nice in a comic book, but in life is pretty fattening and...well, silly looking!

"We went through the comics and saw the basic idea of the character. We decided she was really a 'biker chick'... a 'futuristic, bounty-

Above and opposite: Preliminary designs for Barb's outfit

hunting, sex-pot chick'. In the comics she goes in disguise more, wears some dresses, she's a little more down-scale. I think we've made her more up-scale in the movie. We've glamourised her a bit, which you need to do. The comic is very gritty, the film is more stylised."

The Triumph motorcycle returns to Hollywood (below) – a reminder of other biker-rebel icons such as James Dean and Marlon Brando

Barb rides an impressive motorcycle, with hidden extras. The process of creating the 'Tiger' for the big screen involved meeting with the bike's original manufacturer, Triumph: "Triumph showed us different bikes and we chose, with the director, the most appropriate. Then we discussed how to adapt the scripted features, while not making the rider uncomfortable. Manageability, easy use, visual aspects of the gizmos etcetera were accorded with John Gray, the FX Supervisor. The same goes for the bread truck and the Congressional cars."

As any designer (or, for that matter, the average person in the street) knows, styles and fashions change faster than you can blink. *Barb Wire* may be futuristic in content, but it had to contain styles and images that a contemporary audience would find appealing and sexy. It was up to Rosanna to tread that line very carefully.

"You put shoulder pads on somebody and you're doomed!" Rosanna laughs. "Two years later and you'll look like an idiot, you have to be really careful. I follow fashion in order to avoid it. Whatever's popular at the moment probably won't be when a film comes out up to a year later. Whatever is highly fashionable and exclusive will be available at The Gap stores by then."

Rosanna Norton and Jean-Philippe Carp needed to collaborate closely in their ideas, as she explains:

"We always work closely together. You have to. You don't want someone's costume to be the same colour as the wallpaper. You have to co-ordinate. Jean-Philippe was great and we had a good time working together, and you always have to talk to the actors. My name

may be up there, but they are the ones that are carrying the movie. They have to be comfortable and feel it's right. It's a collaborative thing. You talk to the actors, the director...Pamela is great. She liked the clothes we picked so much that she'd take them home and wear them. She also had ideas for accessories.”

Accessories? That's one way of describing one of the things that Pamela used to get into her role – but Rosanna had no choice in this instance:

“She now has her own real barbed wire tattoo around her arm! I was really surprised when she did that, most actresses don't throw themselves into the part quite that much. We went up to her house to fit her, during pre-production. I nearly fainted when I saw it. We were just going to paint it on her for the movie. It's actually beautiful and quite subtle, but you wonder what will happen when she plays other roles. I think the people at *Baywatch* just use some special make-up to cover it.”

Many of the costumes in the movie were based on outfits that you can't buy just anywhere. This led to some interesting encounters.

“We went out and got a lot of leather. Actually, we had to go into the most terrible stores, the ones that sell all kinds of sex things. We just shot the title sequence and the director suddenly decided that Barb should have a rubber dress on – so that we could reflect the titles in the rubber in a James Bondish way. We had to run and scramble to get rubber dresses in one day. They don't have them everywhere. We found a store that specialised in bondage gear and went in and got one. We got some funny looks. 'Oh...it's for a movie, eh?...*Sure* it is! Would you like to look at our hand-cuffs as well?' I kind of gave up on telling them about the movie in the end!”

Creating an atmosphere is as important as any stunt or effect, as with the street scene above

Words on a page, coupled with a good imagination, can create wonderful images. To transfer those ideas and images onto the cinema screen is a little bit more tricky. A script may describe a huge fire-fight with exploding buildings and mass destruction, but a film's budget, schedule and the laws of physics may deem it unviable. And there is a limit to how far a stuntsperson is willing to go to make a shot look good!

One of the men who tries to get the most bangs for a buck is John Gray, the Special Effects Co-ordinator. His job doesn't just mean lasers and explosions, though. Effects can be as simple as creating the smoke-filled rooms of the Hammerhead and co-ordinating the best way to shoot a scene for a required 'effect'.

"Sometimes you have to work for a long time on an effect that (we'll be lucky if) lasts three to five seconds!" he admits.

"As the Co-ordinator, I have to interact with the director, the producers and decipher exactly what the script is and help the director and then technicians decide how to go about getting those effects to work on set. A part of our job is in creating the style of the film, the atmospheric details with which we have to work.

"The first script that I got was just all-out action. I didn't know what the budget was, but I did know that if they wanted to do all that it would take at least three months preparation before we began filming and probably four times the budget. They knew they couldn't possibly shoot the film according to that first script, but they were basically asking me what I could and could not do."

One scene that had to be worked out carefully was near the climax of the film where Pryzer runs the fork-lift truck into Barb's motorcycle, pinning her so that she cannot escape. That's followed by the crane sequence. Part of this was shot with actors pretending to slug it out high above the ground. Later, scenes were shot with Pamela Anderson and Steve Railsback themselves (slightly less high, but still safely secured). For that type of effect and stunt, Gray

Pam discusses a scene with director David Hogan

worked with the stuntspeople to see what had to be shot with doubles and what could be shot with the actual actors.

As with most of the jobs of pre-production, the duties are far from over when the cameras begin to roll. Preparation is one thing, but it's an on-going process once the film starts.

Direction

Chosen to direct the film was David Hogan. *Barb Wire* is his first time as actual Director of a feature film, though he has an extensive resume of music videos to his credit including work with Diana Ross, Bonnie Raitt, Rod Stewart and Melissa Etheridge. He also won two MTV Awards for Prince's video 'U Got The Look'.

"I had talked to the guys at Dark Horse about *Barb Wire* while I was still working on *Batman*. I was on my way home from a shoot and Steve Tolin called me and asked if I would be able to take on the project." Hogan explains. "I met with him on the Saturday

Udo Kier gets ready for his next shot, with David Hogan

afternoon and began on the Monday.

"I wanted to go for strong colours. I took more from what I did on *Batman* than anything I'd done in my music videos."

Pamela herself has high praise for Hogan. "When David came along, with his finesse and beauty and the way he shoots everything with great art and cinematography...it's brilliant. You can't look bad with this guy. The angles, the shots – it looks like a $50m movie that they're shooting for half the budget!"

Jean-Philippe Carp recalls:

"When David Hogan came in, we were just finishing the bar construction. We walked through and I explained why it was that way. Hogan listened to me and we went back to the office. He just told me: 'Those sets are *your* babies, do what you want, I trust you.' I often say to the people I'm working with: Don't bring a director your questions, bring him your answers."

Action & Location

In big productions, or those that require a great deal of filming to take place in a short time, it is often necessary to have more than one 'unit' shooting at the same time. While one scene is being filmed on a sound stage, another can be up and running on location.

Barb Wire's Second Unit Director is M.James Arnett who also takes the role of Stunt Co-ordinator.

"I came on board at the very beginning of the project. They had signed Pamela and we started looking for shooting locations. The film started shooting and I think it was about a week and a half or so later when we started shooting the second-unit stuff."

Barb Wire used a number of locations for filming, both internally and for external shots:

"We shot essentially at the old Hughes Aircraft plant which was where a lot of the

work was originally done on his Spruce Goose. Those huge old hangers became our stages. Some of it was shot in an old steel mill in Fontana, California, which is a place where films have been shot to death, but it's also a place where they are taking apart and dismantling. Now I understand that there's going to be a huge auto racing track there, so we were probably the last film to shoot there. We shot the warehouse sequence [the film's climax] at South West Marina, San Pedro. There were other smaller locations. In December we went up to the desert for a couple of days for some final shots."

He also explains why filming in the correct locations and conditions is an essential part of the process.

"It's a team effort. If I know they are needing to build a building that then has the side of it

Even props need careful work...before being smashed to bits!

blown out with people near it, then that's the sort of thing that comes down to me. I have to decide how to construct it and talk with other people, such as the design department, the construction people. They may say it can't be done that way. So we can't shoot the way it's written, otherwise it would create a domino effect. Because we talk about stuff like that early on, we usually avoid those problems."

Schedules... and other ideals

There were scheduling problems which no-one could have forseen. Early on in the shoot, newspapers around the world reported that Pamela Anderson was pregnant. Then, when she apparently suffered a miscarriage, the press carried the story with just as much gusto. She recovered quickly, but by the time she returned from some more *Baywatch* duties she was pregnant again. Not only that but co-star Victoria Rowell was also pregnant!

"It did cost us some time, but what could we do, after all it was a little out of our control. We did know up-front that Victoria was pregnant. She was terrific and ready to do anything that she could. The thing was, we didn't really have a realistic schedule, we kept having to go back again and again. It wasn't without its problems, but we got by," said M.James Arnett.

"There were times when I was doing eighteen-hour days, twelve-hour days. It was the hardest thing I've ever done in my life, but it's the most rewarding," Pamela agrees.

"It has been a long shoot, " David Hogan admits. "It's not a fun way to make movies, but it's not unusual for a production to shut down for a couple of

weeks, shoot for another couple, shut down for a week and then start up again for a last couple of weeks. That's a regular story with television. But I can live with it."

Action and FX

It's fair to say that Mr Arnett's job on the Second Unit involves shooting a lot of the action sequences which you see in the movie, the scenes that audiences are most likely to remember. "It's fun to do, it's exciting and you go away really feeling that you've contributed something," he agrees.

Like most fantasy movies (and some contemporary movies where the results are sometimes even more cleverly disguised), visual effects play a big part. How else can you put Barb in the middle of explosions and see Pryzer's inevitable demise to best effect? Arnett admits that such effects require a lot of co-operation.

"On most pictures today there is a Visual Effects Co-ordinator or Post-Production Co-ordinator who is involved from the beginning and it's his job to determine what you are going to need effects-wise. There's nobody's job in this business that is solely his job. Everybody gets involved. In this case, we knew what we needed optically and what was going to be done or be computer generated. There is a bigger array of tools and possibilities today. I think it becomes more of a function of communication.

"We put the actors (rather than doubles) in wherever we could. Wherever you can safely do it, you really need to do it. That's true of whatever film you do. Part of the way to do that is optically. For example to get Pryzer on the fork-lift as it falls was done by the First Unit with a blue screen and then optically, we shot the background 'plates' to match. When you can't get the actors in real time, that's the way to do it.

"Today, you're only limited by time and money. You really can create, visually, just about anything that you can think of given enough time and enough money. It may involve a whole series of technical expertise, but there's not much you can't do!"

"I would say that we managed to do a lot of stuff on set and use computers to enhance it later – rather than just rely on computers for the effect themselves," says David Hogan. "Though there were a few matte shots, a few composites, this isn't really what you would really consider an 'effects movie'. We actually only have as many special effects as, perhaps, the average, straightforward drama. Most of the effects were just done using the camera itself."

Long after her preliminary design work is finished, approved and actually brought to life, Rosanna Norton's chores are still far from over. Costumes and dressing need constant revision, repair and redesign.

"We had to make all of Pam's clothes. After all, she's not a person who walks right into a specific size. Also, everyone has different sizes of shoes. Barb wears high-heeled biker boots. When the

doubles came in we realised that they needed sizes ranging from 6 to size 11. It was hard to keep up with what was needed at a given time. There were so many doubles – a bike-riding double, a high-kicking double. Pam did a lot of her own stuff, but it was more of a scheduling problem. She was sick during the shoot [when she had the miscarriage] so the shooting schedule was re-arranged. Also no-one knew how long the shooting would take. We were still filming the last couple of 'pick-up' shots in December."

The various 'doubles' created a headache in other ways.

"There's a big fight scene where Pamela comes out disguised as a prostitute. Then she gets involved in the huge fight. We had four or five doubles for her. One of them could really kick high, one could shoot the guns – then she got sick, at one point, so we needed a double for the double! At one point we had five people working, including Pamela, and we only had three pairs of the black lace-up gloves that reach half way

up your arm. We never thought we'd have that many doubles. We just sat around taking them off one person and lacing them onto someone else. I wouldn't have chosen those gloves in the first place if I'd known we'd run into that problem."

Endings

Obviously, the climax to any movie is important. If it drags on too long, is over too quick, it spoils the enjoyment, and no matter how good the action was before, the audience is left cheated. For this reason it's particularly important to get everything right, and that depends on finance, time and a little imagination.

"The ending of the movie changed several times, even before Adam left," Arnett explains. "I didn't like the original ending. I thought it had all been done before. It was simply a shoot-out. The first version was simply a foot chase which ended in the warehouse in a gun battle. There was a fight on a hoist and Pryzer just falls to his death. We came up with the ending using the cranes and all of that while we were there on location. David wanted to use the cranes, but make it even bigger. The problem was that it got prohibitively expensive. So we went back to the end that you'll see in the picture. I think it works pretty well."

"I wanted something to bring Temeura back into it at the end. We basically decided to make it bigger than the original ending where it was just Pryzer and Barb," Hogan agrees.

The final pick-up shots of *Barb Wire* were finished about a week before Christmas 1995. Sure, it had been a long and event-filled shoot, but it did mean that the principal cast and crew were finished before the Christmas holidays. Pamela Anderson could take things a little easier, Temeura was off to film *The Island of Dr Moreau* with Marlon Brando, Rosanna Norton was busy designing for the *Brady Bunch* sequel. No rest for the wicked.

How to celebrate the end of the shoot? Even before the end of shooting, Pamela already had something a little novel in mind. "I think for a 'wrap' present, I'm going to have some expert body-piercers in my trailer and whatever the cast want to get pierced...it's on me!"

With that the post-production tweaking starts. It will now be up to the editors, sound mixers, producers and publicity company to shape the movie and decide what works best. That is a process that will not be fully completed until shortly before *Barb Wire*'s release. Like many films, some scenes may be added or deleted for the finished version to provide a movie that runs smoothly and keeps the audience on the edge of their seats. Then there is a whole new set of decisions: What's the best time to release the film? What will the poster be like? Will cast members be available to travel and promote the movie? Will there be a 'Making of...' book? (Yes, you're reading it!)

Barb Wire has been a team effort all the way. From writers and designers to directors and producers, from actors to stuntspeople. Hundreds of people are responsible, in their own way, for bringing *Barb Wire* to the screen. We (and they) hope you enjoy it!